JUDAH'S LION

poems by
ANNE CASTON

Toad Hall Press
North Haverhill, New Hampshire

Printed in Austin, TX, by Morgan Printing.
Author photograph by Abe Alongi.
Cover photograph by Michael H. Piper.
The text of this book is composed in Garamond Premier Pro.

Second Edition

1 2 3 4 5 6 7 8 9 0

Library of Congress Control Number: 2009922585

ISBN: 978-0-915380-71-8

Manufactured in the United States of America

Published by:
Toad Hall Press
2330 Benton Road
North Haverhill, NH 03774

CONTENTS

JUDAH'S LION

continued

THE STORY I SOMETIMES TELL MYSELF:

continued

HOUSE OF GATHERING

Acknowledgments

Grateful acknowledgment is made to the following publications in which these poems, or earlier versions of them, were published:

A Call To Nursing: "The Good We Do"
Annals of Internal Medicine: "Anatomy 101"
Atlanta Review: "Purgatory"
The Long Journey: Pacific Northwest Poets: "House Of Gathering,"
    "Lessons From The Natural World," and "Departures: Last Flight
    From Fairbanks"
The Bread Loaf Anthology of New American Poets: "Blowing Eggs,"
    "Gathering At The River," and "The Burden"
Gargoyle: "What Seems To Be"
The George Washington Review: "The Stone Boy," "Good Friday," and
    "Amen"
Alaska Quarterly Review: "How It Goes"
Maryland Millennial Anthology: "What I Am Waiting For"
Prairie Schooner: "Psalm, After The Fall From Remission," and
    "The Good We Do"
River Styx: "The Body Of An Unidentified Woman Is Retrieved From
    The Jordan"
The Southern Poetry Review: "The Visitation"
Sundog: The Southeast Review: "Rosetta" and "Waiting For You, Father"
Sustenance & Desire: "Psalm, For The Wayside"
Why Are We In Iraq?: "Even In Hell Our Shadows Would Be Eloquent"
    and "At The Moment Of Departure, Each Gesture Fixes Itself"

I am grateful to the National Endowment for the Arts for the generous support it provided for this project; to The George Washington University and the Jenny McKean Moore Fund for a year of writing time and good fellowship; and to the University of Alaska, Anchorage for arranging a workload that was also amenable to a writing life. I also owe a debt of gratitude to good friends, near and far, whose encouragement has sustained me through the writing: David Bradley, Stacey Lynn Brown, Derick Burleson, Grace Cavalieri, Lucille Clifton, Arlitia Jones, Jo-Ann Mapson, Laura Orem, Sherry Simpson, David Stevenson and Kathleen Tarr. I owe a great debt to Maria van Beuren and Toad Hall Press for redeeming this book from the fire and bringing it honorably back into print. Finally, a special thanks to Dorianne Laux for her generous suggestions and insights on some of these poems, and to Janna Rademacher, good friend and publicist through the good times and the tough. *Grazie.*

Foreword

"Where, among the ordinary every-day/goings-on,
begins the moment of disaster?" — Anne Caston

Raw and relentless, the poems in *Judah's Lion* are about suffering, and
about endurance, and about our capacity to face, again and again, "the
whole thorn-torn mess a world can sometimes be." A native of Ar-
kansas and a former nurse, Anne Caston stands next to those in pain,
in extremity, stays with them through the first days and during the
final moments, leans in close and listens. She sneaks a dying patient
a last cigarette, cares for the damaged, buries the "half-made," locks
eyes with the sundered, and considers herself lucky, the kind of luck
found in knowing how to do the difficult thing that needs to be done.

Judah's Lion is a pleasure to read, intelligent, moving, grap-
pling, as it does, with reason and faith, daring to tell the stories
of those of us at "the frayed rope-end of hope." Nothing is won
or lost easily in this book: war, love, the struggle with spirit, with
fury. Read "The Stone Boy," "Bleak Pond," "That You Are, Likely,
Not Created in God's Image," "Conversation With My Body,"
read "That This Is How It Begins," and "Lessons From The Natu-
ral World." These poems are not pretty, though the language
used to make them sings with its own beauty; rather they are real
things, sharp stones wrenched up out of the lived life of the poet.

Dorianne Laux

For Ian, always, my love and gratitude,
and for Matthew, my son,
whose story this also is.

What Seems to Be

Sometimes the life I am living
    resembles the life I seem to be living.
Sometimes. But mostly not. Mostly
    the mornings rise, shrouded
in mist, the brook over-running the rocks, wind
    shuffling and sighing in high pines.
I see these things, but they are no use to me
    nor am I any use to them.
When lamps are lit in the dark
    house at night, I am unmoved
by them though they flicker and flare
    and, finally, fall.
And when the stars hold out
    their torches against the darkness I am
indifferent to them too, though I once believed
    if I didn't care for things, they might
forsake me or cease to be. But no;
    the days pass, and the nights, as ever.

Once I let a stranger steal a chicken from my yard.
    I watched him slip back into shadows
and thorns at the wood's edge, grinning at his luck.
    He washed up, next day, downstream, throat slashed.
Coroner told me he'd opened the man
    and found roast chicken undigested in his gut.
Where, he asked, *does a vagrant find food like that?*
    Dunno, I shrugged, though he knew I did.
He shook his head and invited me in
    to have a look at the body.
Whoever cut him, cut him
    good: from ear to ear.
Almost took his head off.

This afternoon, I pour myself
some sweet tea over ice, sit down, put my glasses on,
    and write it all down for you.
As if that is the proper thing to do. As if
    I have some right to it.

JUDAH'S LION

The Visitation

All Hallow's Eve, Opelika, Alabama, 1979

Ah, here is Time — ticking and grim, thin
    tin-foil sickle in hand — and the Holy

Ghost, white as a dove in his bleached bedsheet.
    And, on their heels: Death, come knocking.

I step out, eight months large and awkward, bearing sweet
    treats to appease the boyish bent towards trickery.

Up the flagstone walkway behind them, singing, comes
    Ophelia in her best pink ballet shoes and bridal

gown, in her brindled eyes that bottomwater look.
    Last I saw her was mid-July, on 4 a.m. rounds:

pale, both wrists bound to the bedrails, her
    wide eyes Lithium-lit, her twin

barely two days dead. *Called home*
    to be with his Lord. So said the priest

though we all knew he'd drowned
    in the family well. Of his own accord. To hell

with the Lord. Or the Devil. Or whatever
    crazed hatter'd made him madder than most.

Put out the light please, she'd pleaded,
    so I can find my way skyward to him.

So I put out the overhead light and I saw
    how some parent or nurse or well-meaning

aide had glued glow-in-the-dark stars
    to the ceiling of the Children's Ward.

And now arrives my neighbor's lame-legged boy — slow-witted too,
    as if one blow were not sufficient — lurching up,

unmasked, his fake face cracked and dangling
    at his throat from its thin noose of elastic.

He nearly topples Time in the breathless rush
    to pull back his collar, waistband and sleeves,

to show where his mother's penned D-O-N-N-I-E
    on all his clothes and that paper sack

from which a slack-jawed jack-o'-lantern grins.
    In case I lose myself again, the boy explains.

Ophelia blinks and grins and takes
    his sticky hand in hers, both of them

softening then in the porchlight among the night's horrors.
    Death and Time and God excuse themselves

so all the sweetness I have left gets heaped upon these
    not-well-finished ones who thank me well and turn

and vanish too like some unnamed doubled
    constellation appearing then flickering out.

The Stone Boy

Before the diagnosis was confirmed
I knew it, knew from the night of his birth, knew
when I lifted first the blue bundle of his body
and he arched — a wild thing, roaring,
bloody still — and clenched himself against me.

I knew it too in the long night hours
when hunger roused him in his cradle:
I'd find him fretting, one wet fist shoved
against his mouth, though when I tried to nurse him
he tightened and went rigid in my arms.

I learned to leave him
tangled in damp sheets, to lean
an arm's-length off, to bottle-feed warmed
milk, to watch 'til, full and drowsy, he'd drift
beyond his need again, and mine.

In the second year: that midnight
din of banging in the house; I'd race the stairs to find
him upright, bumping hard, the wall behind him crumbling.
One night, he rocked his crib to pieces; just in time, I found
him, hung and blue, where he'd fallen through the tipped mattress.

One afternoon when he was three, napping among picnic leavings
and a new toy boat he'd smashed, I turned from him; I walked out
into the muddy Chattahoochee, skirt, shoes, and all; it too
refused me. But I ask you: what mother would drown herself, her boy
asleep nearby? And what would happen to the child, waking,
blinking in the noonday sun, near such a wild current as that?

I've come to believe he is the fierce
rock of my own hard heart coming back at me.
The apple doesn't fall far from the tree.
I've heard it; so have you.
He's mine, isn't he?

Still, I wish I could say that some nights,
standing in the boy's room, watching him,
small and quiet in his bed as he stared off past me,
past the turning stars and moons and planets of the mobile,
past the grinning bear and tin soldier and the red kite he sometimes liked,
I wish I could tell you I almost forgot my terror long enough to love him.

Good Friday

For days now, nothing but fevers and fits, the bittersweet
mete of madness. I almost leave the boy home,
for fear of how he might be among the devout
Catholics of the town for whom this is a holy day.
But they are done with him now, his fits; the deep
blue bruises of exhaustion widen under his eyes;
he grows drowsy and calm again. So I pack
a blanket and we set off, hand in hand, for a rise
at the edge of town. We could be almost any
mother and son ascending a sun-riddled slope
where believers gather, Bibles and prayerbooks in hand.

The pageant begins: a path of palm fronds
criss-crosses and climbs the steep-raked hill.
Priests in white and two weeping women
follow the cross to which is nailed
a statue of the Suffering Savior.

He rises then, all four troubled years of him, swaying
on the wide worn blanket we share, his
dark eyes fastened to that crucifix.
When he's got it by heart, the boy
throws out his arms and drops his head.
I hear stunned gasps around us
on the hillside. All through that noonday
procession, through the sad slow hymns,
while the saints carry again their burden
to the top of Golgotha, the boy holds — fixed
as He was once — between earth and sky.

Amen

Mad as a hatter. Certifiable. Surely that's what they think,
strangers who see him in the midst of his fits and turn fast away.
Except one woman in the park today

who offers up a prayer: *Lord, have mercy on this boy.*
He's never been one to pray — no
now-I-lay-me-down for him — though he likes

to loudly shout *Amen* at the end of someone else's prayers.
Like Sundays, when the Doxology's sung
over the collected tithes: the boy will sometimes rise

from the pew — clapping and spinning
in the aisle — to howl like a radio preacher:
Ay-men. Ay-men. Dance for Jesus

and all His shiny pennies. Lord of the Dance,
how You must love the boy for that.
What moves me is his music.

It begins, late nights, as humming — a little
melody, no words — and grows to equal
whatever comes over him there in the sleepless dark.

Humming. Then words, a song from some deep
well in him: *Come in, ye wildebeest, come in.*
Lie beside my bed. There are no lions here.

And on like that until all singing falls,
in the end, to his one favorite word:
amen... amen... amen....

Tonight the fever's on him again and, while he's fiercely
singing, down the dark corridor something pierces me —
pity or deep grief — as I make my way

down the hall to kneel beside his bed.
I ease down, my head next to his on the pillow.
The wildebeest again?

He nods. *He's sad, he is always so sad.*
I understand. Or think I do. I try to tell him so
but he places one damp hand over my mouth

like some old conspirator. *I like
his shaggy head*, he whispers
against my ear, *and the mud on his mouth.*

Well, and haven't I learned by now to take
what music is given me? We'll stay like this
'til daybreak: a boy humming to himself, to his beast,

and a woman who waits again in the darkness
under a son's wet palm, under the double blade of his little
psalms and what God hath delivered, this time, into her hands.

Purgatory

for Dr. John Gimbel

You spoke of it once as a place between
    closed doors the no-longer-living
come to, kept company for a time
    by the souls of infants. But I
say it's a hospital nursery in Alabama,
    full-windowed, but with drapes pulled
day and night and a door at either end: one
    by which you enter, the other a red-lit exit.
In that nursery each midnight, three women
    in white: angels of the interstices, waiting
for some final synapse to fire, for one door

    or the other to swing wide on its hinge.
Some nights it seemed as if
    the place had revolving doors,
so quickly did so many pass
    in and out again. One
boy – a hydrocephalic infant
    whose mother had left him behind – was
assigned to me. How long now before I can forget
    the heavy-headed heft of him: that swollen cranium
cradled in my left palm as he drank? Impossible
    to hold him like other babies:

the head might pitch or roll and the pearl-thin
    vertebrae of the neck might snap
under the head's sudden weight. Or those eyes
    which would not, *could not*, close
even in deepest sleep, even in the heavy
    undertow of anæsthesia? While I cannot say
I was repulsed by him, I also can't say that
    I cared for him beyond what was required of me.

For ten nights, I rocked and fed him, lifting
    and lowering him into and out of the warm
heart of the isolette.

    Ten midnights, I checked his shunt; I listened
to his heart and lungs; I thumped his left sole, then his right.
    Ten nights I flooded those pale open pupils with light
and watched for unequal constriction. He was nothing
    to me, that shunned one of the nursery, that
unwieldy doll in a hospital tee shirt and diaper.
    Nothing, that is, 'til the three a.m. hour
in which something in him fired and failed and he sank
    though I worked — though all three of us did —
to clear the shunt, to breathe for him, to pull him back
    from that far door though some wiser, fiercer thing in me
kept insisting, *let go... let go....*

The Good We Do

To loosen, a little, the girdle
in which death had cinched a man I knew,
I left my midnight charting and stole from the nurses' station.
Nothing strange in that, nothing
anyone would question.

Everything about my long walk down that darkened hall
seemed right and, at the same time, wrong.
Sterile walls shone in the half-light; fresh
wax gleamed and squealed under my soles.
On the door to the man's room

a new sign: *No CPR.*
Well, then.
So be it.

I stepped past the sleeping wife.
Such things are easy enough to do.
I turned the oxygen off and loosed the mask
that had strapped him to the flow.
Beside the bed, a Gomco gurgled noisily.

He gurgled too in the sludge of lungs gone bad.
I shook him: he startled, and would've cried out,
but I held the forbidden thing close enough
he could make out what it was
in the dulled streetlight from the window.

I placed it on the bedside tray.
Back in five, I whispered, and stepped outside
to wait. I didn't want to watch.

It's strange, don't you think, how the good we do
we do loudly. But our sins?
Those we ease into in secret, and quietly.
And quietly was how I waited in that dim hallway.
Not for five, but for ten full minutes.

I eased back past the woman who was bruised with exhaustion
and watching over him. I thought he, too, had drifted off.
But when I turned to leave, he sat up, took my hands in his,
and blessed me, hard, for what I'd done. My hands
stung from the fervor of his blessing.

He rested well that night
and died some days later,
as we'd expected.

One cigarette. It was the singular kindness I could give,
though even that was wrong. I know that; I knew it then.
But the needle he'd begged for – "to end the pain" –
I couldn't give him that. Not that. Not
coward that I was.

I tell you this today, not to confess, not to
clear my conscience. I say it so it's clear to you
I believe I might be living yet
because of the furious blessing
he bequeathed to me that night.

I say it so you'll know
how it is that I have come to live
deeply in the shadow of my own guilt

and an old misplaced sense of mercy
which – despite anything
I might once have told you otherwise –
has at its center for me still
an odd, fierce comfort.

Judah's Lion

Irony is beyond a boy like mine. As is symbolism.
    Allegory. Metaphor too. All is literal with him
        though that doesn't rule out a wildebeest,
the one he meets each morning in the fallow field
    beyond our yard, the one who lies beside him
        each night now in the dark.

Some mornings the boy stands a long time, one hand
    shading his eyes, looking sunward, scanning the wide
        sky for that fiery wheel – Ezekiel's wheel – *way up*
in de middle ob de air. He says he'd like to see that
    himself. Just once. If the sun would
        get out of the way.

God has a lamb, he tells me one night after prayers,
    who followed Jesus to school just like Mary's
        lamb in the Mother Goose book.
And God? God, for him, is just one giant eye *roaming to and fro*
    over the dark earth, peering through windows at night
        like some neighborhood peeping Tom.

To him, a fiery wheel is a wheel in flames, a lamb a lamb, an eye
    an eye, and as of this morning's sermon, the Lion
        of Judah – *coming again, and the unholy*
shall be judged and torn – is an orange cat that belongs to Judah
    Michaels, a boy who lives two doors down.
        "I will kill that lion if he comes near," he mutters,

pocketing stones and pebbles as he walks all afternoon the gravel drive
    between our house and Judah's, the young tom pouncing
        bugs in the weed-riddled grass of the Michaels' front yard.

But now, the Sunday sun is almost spent and we settle
together on the splintered back stoop while shadows
creep forward from the field where his wildebeest waits.

While fireflies sputter on and off and crickets
call out across the twilit lawn, he is telling me now
about Zion, that *beautiful city of God,* which is
somewhere, he says, in Georgia, near Stone Mountain
except everything there — streets, people, trees — has gone
gold as Christmas glitter. God's people, he says,

are marching, *marching upward to Zion,* and he tilts
the stick he's holding to show me how steep is the climb.
He's going there too one day, he says, when he is big,
when he is old, when he must leave me. I stare at the darkening
field, considering again the lilies, the wildebeest I cannot see,
the whole thorn-torn mess a world can sometimes be.

Who wouldn't long for a Zion like his: the sky gone fiery, bright
overhead as Ezekiel's wheel, Gabriel singing us home
to Georgia again, this boy and me and his wildebeest,
all of us marching up, up God's glittering mountain
where the Lamb of God and the Lion of Judah
lie down together and wait for us

there, somewhere in the polished hard and shining future.

The Hunt

1.

What my son wants most is a monarch — *Danaus*
plexippus — but he is sick today so I go
in his place, early morning, fingering
the vacant undersides of the dew-damp
milkweed of the north pasture,
etherized jar in hand.

Where the monarch will repose: a wide emptiness waits.
The boy means it to hover there, he tells me, *always,*
as if in perpetual flight, gold wings unfurled, rimed
with black, and the two tell-tale
spots of a male.

For ten days now he has scouted out the waxy jade
of a last chrysalis crowned with gold, watching
as it grows translucent, the monarch's body
swelling with stored blood. *A monarch*
needs blood, he says. *To inflate its wings.*

2.

When blood in the wings dries
stiff, the monarch can fly.
Until then, he's just so much
bright baggage
slung from a twig of birch.

Only the briefest moment exists
in which to capture the prize.
Too quick, the wings stay furled
forever, the abdomen bloated as a bee's.
Too slow, the monarch takes flight.

3.

But today in the field, something's gone
queer: through the sheared chrysalis
a white smudge struggles free:
albino. Aberration
of nature. Two wings inflate

and before me again rises last night's
x-ray and its white butterfly, dead-
center of the girl: two wide wings
where her heart and lungs had ruptured
from the concussion of the suicide

bomb — a pale smear riddling the black
sky of her body like the arrival of some strange
comet, some first odd sign
against the darkness in her
where all the wrong stars had lined up.

Anatomy 101

What I remember now are the animals: pithed
frogs, fetal pigs, and cats – so many cats – rubbery and reeking
of formaldehyde. Slowly they dissolved, under our hands,
one system at a time, until just stiff carcasses remained,
their former animal eloquence stripped down to rank
bone and sinew. God, how the place stank.

Only one was ever otherwise: a Shepherd pup
who entered on a long leash, wagging and drooling,
fresh-sprung from the local pound.
We made a circle around him; we ran our hands
over his rough head and ears. We said, *Good boy!*
and *What's his name?* and *Is he pure-blooded?*

Our instructor commanded the dog, *Sit!* – and he did.
And he went, just like that, still slobbering,
still panting for joy, into those hands. The needle went in,
clean; the dog slumped and fell, sidewise, onto the steel
dissecting table where we were circled still around the dead
beast, like Stonehenge, our shamed and secret faces turning inward.

The Burden

By the time I got to them, the woman was stoned
    on sorrow and half a jar of gin; her man,
cold sober, was praying and casting out demons.
    On the kitchen table, a box: a doll
dressed for burial. On the ashy hearth nearby, the dead
    child swaddled in a filthy towel.

I stooped to see: again, a son,
    third one in three years to arrive half-made.
A *changeling,* the man called him, *the Devil's
    work in a woman's womb.* He left off
the exorcism of her body long enough
    to tell me: *Throw it, like the others, to the dogs.*

They'll not touch the body again, not even
    to dispose of it; that's why I'm called, three times now.
No sin for me to lift the damaged and dead.
    Lord knows, I've done worse. So I folded
the boy back into his rags and left with him
    slung in the crook of my arm.

I threw the dogs, starved as they were, the blood-caked
    afterbirth and cord, then drove seven miles west
to a rotting trestle hung out over a gorge.
    I slid down the mud-slick slope to the swollen
banks of the creek where I pulled back the reeking rags
    to have, in the bright morning light, a better look.

I tell you, it shook me a little, the sight:

that translucent fetal skin, all the veins
    visible and cursive, like something penned
in an indecipherable hand and, under the milky lids, two

yellow orbs — no pupils, no irises. Ten fingers; ten toes.
And when I rolled him over, near the base
    of the skull, the blue-gray brain bulged.

Worse: the rot and ooze down the under-
    belly and along the swollen sex.
When I stooped to the shallows, to rinse the body
    of birth's debris, some of the skin washed
free of the bones; so I lifted what was left of the boy
    and laid him down in the dew-drenched grass.

I tore the ruined linen three times down its length,
    knotted the ends together, and wound it, whole-cloth,
'round the body, head to toe, binding a stone in as I went.
    I tied it off with a double knot, breathed
a blessing over it, and cast the bundle out into the stream:
    it bobbed twice and went under; it surfaced again.

Then it sank and was gone for good.

In this lies the burden of lifting to light
    from the squalor of this world
what is — or is almost — undone: that
    a straw doll can be blessed and laid to rest
under a white-washed cross on which is carved *Boy*
    Tolbertson, while the syphilitic's son drifts — as he has now

for twenty-two years — through the dream-riddled
    nights of the rest of my life: a changeling,
in his milky skin and his rough-knotted shroud, moving
    beyond minnows and old moorings
and my meager blessing towards the sea
    and his other lost brothers.

Beseeching The Lord Of Tooth And Claw

Lord, it's true: I have interfered
in matters that were none of my business.
I have pounded bad hearts back to life and buried three
boys in a river. I have studied the darkness
between two candles and plundered the Book
of the Dead. I have said the best
way to break a stutterer is to
teach him to lie or pray.

~

But will You not answer me now,
O One-Who-Has-Torn-and-Departed?

~

After the August rains, the night turns
strange: a mauve moon rising
and, on earth, the deepening
shadows in which things lose themselves.

In a lantern-lit room, my
son, cracked compass, drifts,
furled in the gauze-white sail of fever,
downriver to disaster or death.

~

Beyond the darkened yard, rising bright in the forest's
black heart: Destroying Angel and the Death Cup.
He came to this world, a half-drowned thing.
Weary from the long birth-hours, I slept;
his father, when he saw him, wept,
the boy swollen and bruised from the birth-tongs.

But oh, the songs he came here with!
Even the silver spoons of the forceps knew
enough to envy him that.

~

Okay then; You want war?
You be a captain, gilt and glittering; I'll be
a sea-side meadow where children play.
When You point Your long guns
through the fog, what will they be?

~

My father's word for this
is *prayer*. Others say *heresy*.
I call it the heart's last falcon-cry
going out, the soul nailed to the body's
cross, while eternity's sirens sing.

Bleak Pond

All night one winter nearly twenty
    years ago, the generator's lights

burned towards rippled ice
    where a boy had fallen through: we knew

because his hockey stick sailed
    crookedly – half in, half out, tipped

in the frozen wake he'd made – marking
    the place of his going.

I'd been sent to bring his mother 'round
    and had found her huddled, shivering

wildly in her wooly coat and boots– her
    apron underneath – calling her boy's name

over and over. As if, somehow,
    she already knew.

Stew simmered on the stove.
    Four biscuits rose on waxed paper.

    ~

Where, among the ordinary every-day
    goings-on, begins the moment of disaster?

    ~

All night I stood beside her
    rooted in dark drifts

at the pond's rim, though she was drifting
    somewhere beyond me and the light's gaudy glare.

The woods seemed full of nothing
    save her sorrow and snapping ice.

So when a wolf at the ice-white curve of the pond's jaw
    threw back its rough head, unbared its teeth

and wailed, the woman collapsed in a near-dead
    heap at my feet. A fireman likewise

dropped to his knees in the snow.
    Still the furious rescue lights burned

coldly on, as did stars overhead.
    Three rescue workers later swore

an aurora brightened the sky
    when his body was lifted free.

If it did, I didn't see it;
    I was watching something let go

the frayed rope-end of hope in his mother's eyes.
    For once, in those woods, I overlooked

the deer who rushed by and the fox's
    brushy tail. For once I moved, joylessly,

back through spruce and long-limbed birch.
    This morning, twenty-something years

past all of it, the almost-final terror of it
	settled now like facts in a history book,

I'm wondering how that flaming morning-after dared
	to rise as usual and cast its ordinary eye

over the pond, the drowned child, the woman
	staggering homeward again,

as if to just have been there meant
	the bright day could lay claim to any of it.

And how, this morning, dare I?

The Body Of An Unidentified Woman
Is Retrieved From The Jordan

Pulled this morning from the river
    after a long night-search
with lines and ladders, ropes and grappling
    hooks, who is she now having passed
through the waters, washed clean of her despair? Who
    is this one for whom today bells are rung
and the gates of heaven heave?

Maybe somewhere something has saved
    a place for her: an empty chair
at the table, one dog-eared page in a book,
    the black silk slip she dropped.
Maybe a man crossed, all night, the moat
    of her absence and a child cried,
inconsolable, in its cradle.

Maybe there were dances once
    and a blue chiffon gown and a white
orchid pinned to the strap of that gown.
    This morning though, the ruined boat of her
body lies moored in the city morgue and no one comes
    to claim her. The world goes
cleanly on without her.

Gathering At The River

I.

In a thicket this morning, river-hung, a feed sack:
in it, a millstone and twelve gray kittens.

I have loved this river all my life. And, sometimes, the God
who, surely, looked on and did nothing.

II.

My father says God is The Potter
who sets each man, as clay, on a wheel

and makes of him a vessel, which He then perfects
in the great fires of tribulation.

If the firing is done well, that man will endure,
and his faith, as the saints before him

endured their stonings, drownings, boilings-in-oil.
Like in the Book of Martyrs which I saw once as a child:

the righteous in white robes who, though demons gnashed at them,
lifted their eyes to heaven and praised God.

God will, in His own time — so says my father — deliver them.
Joy cometh in the morning.

III.

Shall we gather at the river, the old hymn goes, *gather
with the saints at the river that flows by the throne of God.*

But this river runs to sea and I am no saint this morning,
something in me drowned as these twelve dead

disciples of the sack, drowned
beyond praising anything.

IV.

Potter, after the wheel and fire of this life,
You can cast me off on the banks of this river, a half-wrought

vessel, flawed, some busted cup where the dead are hung: that
music You will hear again when the wind goes, singing, through it.

Lucky

Some humid summer twilight, you're shelling field peas
mindlessly, listening to the *plink* they make as they fall
into the metal colander; or maybe you're sitting
on the splintered stoop in your flour-dusted apron
dreaming of another life, the life you might have had
had you been smart or brave or lucky enough;
maybe you're watching fireflies rise and fall
in the summer-scorched field, humming
the refrain of some old hymn
and that's when you hear it: a sound
from deep in the swamp, like crying,
like something lost and small, but you're not
sure, not exactly, so you leave off what you're doing
and cross the field to stand at the edge of the swamp
until, sure enough, there it is and there's no mistaking it
this time and, for the first time, you believe
those tales about women
stealing, midnights, into the swamp
carrying baskets of blanketed babies — their unwanted
sons, their ruined-from-birth daughters — and though you have,
in your life, been afraid of everything, especially snakes and quicksand,
you know that you cannot, *cannot,* leave that crying thing, whatever it is,
to the merciless swamp; so, despite your terror, you pass
through the palmettos' blades, stooping
under moss-draped cypress and oaks, closer
and closer to that plaintive wail until finally you see something
struggling in the viscous sludge of the chemical plant tailings pond —
something smallish and black as the pitchy swamp-mud save for the whites
of the terrified eyes — only just then he sees you too and howls louder
and struggles in earnest to free himself which is, of course,
the very means by which the quicksand works more quickly,
so you make your way to a fallen bough and crawl along it

and fish him, slippery, out of the foul soup
so you can carry him, reeking and grateful, home
where you hose him down and towel him off and fetch
a bowl of leftover stew which he finishes off before he falls,
full and sighing, into exhausted sleep and that's exactly when you fall
under his charm and since he seems to like you too, you let him stay
and name him – *Lucky* – because it seems he must be
to get a coward like you to come so far to fetch him;

but a dog like that has a thing for bogs so he takes to wandering
again, more and more often, until one day you hear his yelp
and there you are again, deep in the boggy heart of the swamp,
whistling and calling, though he ignores you again as he always does
and that's when you see, with a shiver, the troubled waters of the pond
and know it means there's a crocodile near so you stagger away
and swear to yourself *to hell with that dog*
but you look back then
and that's when you see that
the luckiest thing in your life
has heard, has heeded your call, and is
paddling, happily, towards you, though you see too
how he's only half a dog now – the crocodile's cruel work
done – and suddenly this is what's left to you: this
near-gone thing swimming your way
and you, on solid ground, clapping and calling,
Here, boy! Good dog! Here, boy!
as if nothing is wrong, as if nothing is different than a dozen
afternoons when you coaxed him back home with your voice;
but when he hits the shallows and tries to stand and can't,
you see in his eyes he knows now too
so you step off into the muck disregarding, for once,

the cottonmouths and the crocs and the quicksand
because, such as he is, he is all that you have
and this is something you know how to do;
and that's when you know,
as if for the first time, that you are *not*
someone soured and ruined by sorrow, not
a woman with a stone for a heart; no,
that's when you suddenly see yourself new:
someone who'll enter your most-dreaded
darkness to go after that least thing you love,
someone who'll take back what you can
from the leviathan jaw, because you can see now,
and clearly, how something that reckless and ruined
could both do you in and could save you somehow,
because that's how it goes in this one life you're given,
because *that* is how lucky *you* are.

Rosetta

Because that crooked table in its shaft of sunlight
seemed too bare, too lonely with her mute day after day,
because I was aware then of the sweater, threadbare
at the cuffs, the ragged slippers and the steel-gray
empty of her eyes,
              I brought some flowers
in a glass — a plain one, clear as a cup — to set
between us in that place where sun and silence settled
equally on the rough grain of the table and her hands
which traveled ceaselessly over the splintered wood.
Despite the simple glass, the flowers made a lovely
riot in the dull dayroom.
                 She made
a point of looking, then *over*looking them.
I lifted out a stalk of lavender, pinned it to her
frayed lapel and tucked a bright red poppy over her ear.
She looked through me as if through air, then slumped
and saddened in her chair. So we spent our mandatory hour.
And the next. And so forth, for a month, then two. The flowers
perished early on, as flowers do, and still the sun kept falling
brightly on the table, her unquiet hands, the glass. Fell too
that silence, harsh and unreadable as the scalded
stone of her face.
               Towards Michaelmas, I threw the rotted
flowers out. My ring against the jar made a musical *ping*.
She spoke then, in a loud rush, of a cradle just the hue
and color of that table.
               Twice more, I tapped that
rim; twice more, it rang; she spoke: *Who was it*
held me, face to the fire? Who?
And then: *Tell me, what's so natural*
about it - dying, I mean - and the soul creeping off

to do some deed in solitary without the body?
When she spoke, I went mute, dumb
before the onslaught of her words.
                              Rosetta,
how like that glass between us I've become — I
see that now — a thing, when thumped, that rings
with song, all words a reckless *rushing-after.*

Blowing Eggs

My grandmother taught me the delicate trick:
    to choose a silver pin, to prick
both ends, to put the mouth to it, just so,
    to blow until the insides are blown clear.

What's left in hand is brittle, but more
    amenable to art, to the swab and splash
of color, the varnish, the slick veneer.

    A thing like that could last for years
on some high shelf, outlive the daily scramble
    common things come to in the end.

And the hen who laid the egg?
    My brother and I, in mischief, once slipped
the painted thing beneath her in the nest:
    she shrieked and pecked it to bits.

THE STORY
I SOMETIMES TELL MYSELF:

| *Anne Caston*

That This Is How It Begins

She *isn't*. And then she *is,* waking
into life on a hot May morning.
And God is no more than a sycamore's

shadow between her and a blistering sun.
Thus does she become herself, awkward
trinity of elbows, bony knees, bare feet:

a freckled five-year-old hanging
over fence rails, singing
to her grandfather's gruffest goat.

And all afternoon, dreaming –
such dreaming! – in the wake
of the fan's turning blades. Easy days.

But this is before her body
blossoms into view. Before her
mule-headed mind takes hold of her.

Before she becomes a mutiny in the Sunday pew.
Commandments, commandments
everywhere: *thou shalt not... if thine eye offend....*

Better, they say, to pluck it out
than spend eternity in the flames.
Not sin? Her?

An eye could sooner not blink
than she could not sin.
Thus does she arrive at this

lying in the bed she's made
with a ravening hunger and a womanish body
which, they remind her, is sacred, is

the "temple of God." Remember,
they say to her, in times of temptation,
remember Christ: the Body broken,

the Blood of the Lamb.
She says, to hell with the blood.
Bring on the tender flesh.

That Even Then We Were Marked For Destruction

This is how it *really* begins:
a woman with a future marries
a man with a past.

Rigged, as she always is, to the wrong
mast, to the storm's Atlantic eye,
it seems like destiny to her

when he washes up, a laden wreck
she hauls from the sludge
as if he were loaded with gold.

Hip-deep in the muck, she heaves;
her backbone cracks from his weight.
Beneath her too he is breaking up.

In her agony, she cries out, "Love!"
But he, with his bracken-slick heart, lets go
at last the rough raw hemp of her, slipping

sea-ward again, and he speaks not
even one word of parting
before going under.

That Mirrors Are Not Necessary

Instead of marrying
    a man she loves, she marries
        a man her father approves of,

and all the way to the altar
    and back, through the difficult
        days and nights that follow her

away from there, she says to herself
    through clenched teeth, *Whatever
        it takes... whatever it takes...*

while the rooms of her house grow
    raucous with children, her gardens
        fragrant and reckless,

until one day she can see
    she's become her mother, full of detergent
        and godliness, a decent woman

wondering what could possibly save her now.

That We Live, Mostly, In Another Kingdom and Unto Ourselves

Tonight she considers the ends of things:
    a mind, a marriage, the slim tether-hold on hope.

All rivers, he shouts at her, *run to the sea.*
    She wants to know what they're running from.

Once she owned a key
    to the last, lost door of his heart.

But now the Prince of Twilight fills
    all of his pockets with chains —

this man who wants, each day now,
    to put a bullet in his brain, this man

whose hands have trembled, like a girl's,
    on the buttons of her blouse —

and each hour now, waking
    and sleeping, belongs to shadow-things.

Among the midnight pulleys, a black gull circles.
    Even the clocks run wild.

And his face tonight is not
    the face of any man she has loved.

That Even The Strongest Among Us Can Be Easily Undone

Childhood, for him, is a thrown stone
 sunk into the obsidian
  lake of his past.

Sometimes now, he retrieves it
 just for the satisfaction
  of tossing it away again.

She knows, if his mother had
 her way, she'd bore a hole in it
  and tie it, millstone,

around his neck, a thing
 which could drown him — any day,
  any hour — easily as a sacked cat.

That, In Each Beginning, The End Is Written

The breech calf pulled finally into the near-dawn
    dark, wailing in the hay-sweet barn, and she tells the man

it's as if she has had her hands on the bloody rim of some first morning
    out of which everything once sprang, full-throated as robins,

into being. Not a morning as they understand mornings now: sun
    blazing in over the meadow, dragging them forward

from dreams into each day and its obligations. And not
    the dreaded morning which will one day rise,

apocalyptic, heavy with knowing, over
    the shattered ends of things.

She means that morning which must've stood wide-eyed
    in the circle of itself and didn't yet know

to cry, halfling both to the darkness
    into which it was borne and to the coming light

by which everything else would also arrive
    making too its own strangled song under the opening sky.

That, Sometimes, What You've Wanted Arrives And Takes You In Its Teeth

One night he loves her; the next, he doesn't.
Something's moving in on them — she feels
it — a dark army, a seething
hive, animal parts rotting, a stench
carried toward them on the back of a stiff wind.

No need to speak of pain.

He'll punish them both
enough before he's done: a man
pulling out of himself, hand over fist, and her
standing there in her right mind, holding the fraying rope-
end of love or something like it.

That Every Love Song Becomes, In The End, A Lament

Unfathomable, really: the myriad ways
    one man can ruin himself.

But no man is an island:
    he goes down, she goes too.

Some nights now, she practices
    folding the house of the heart so it will lie

flat and neat and uninhabited
    by the small spiders of need.

But pride is a poor companion
    and the end of the road is poor enough

for one with nothing left to bear
    save the brunt of love.

Yes, *love* — that clean and easy arithmetic:
    what can be added; what can be taken away.

Such grief, such grief, *0 Deus Otiosus!*
    This is why we have funerals, isn't it?

And When Is The Sky Ever Anything But Blue
Over The Disaster Of The Day

She has always loved the sky
    though what she held to and called *sky*
        was only the string-end of the real
            kite of it flying somewhere
                beyond what she could see.

And she has loved the sun
    though she could not fix her eyes
        on it or on the bright combustion
            of its engine driving the earth
                through the green machinery of spring.

She tries some days now
    to imagine it back: a woman,
        a man, a garden, its beasts and, deep
            in the mountain's granite
                heart, the first stone

waiting to be lifted to light.
    But she's seen what a stone can become
        in a hand. The day wobbles wild
            on its delicate spindle, red
                and rotting through, and even

the sky is no refuge now, fierce
    with stars, as if God might suddenly
        hurl himself through, dragging
            the hosts of heaven behind
                bright and burning with vengeance.

That You Are, Likely, *Not* Created In God's Image

If so, it would not move her as it does: the soot-smudged
face of a stranger sifting through rubble there in a far city
where the wrecking-ball of terror has brought tall buildings
down to dust and ash. Nor would it disturb her, his endless
excavation, nor how he steers his weary body home and back again,
navigating a loss which has become the map, the pole-star, compass and
clock by which he'll chart the remainder of his days.

If so, would she concern herself with her own man
or how they fall upon each other savagely now
in the body's terror of *ceasing-to-be?*
And would they matter either, those small daily tragedies — spilt
salt, ruined milk, soured dough — or the blister of love, the heat
and press of it, the iron-clad glove of it thrown down, the gauntlet
run each day to prove she is worthy?

And what would it be to her, the location, the shifting latitude and
longitude of woe, or that wandering girl on the news today
in her dress of splinters, holding fistfuls of forget-me-nots?
And would she be so troubled by the Judas-hearted friend
or the unexpected mercies of strangers or the ordinary
stoop under which the latest tyrant of history sleeps
tonight with his dogs?

If she were some mere mirror-image of God, she would not
heed the brief sweet solace of bees nor the last
refrain of crickets at dusk, wind passing
through pines. Nor would she be so easily torn
or comforted tonight when the boats lower their sails
and the flag comes down and all the bells in town begin
tolling, *Ask not... ask not....*

That If $x = Me$ and $y = You$, We Are Still Not A Fixed Point On Any Plane

A key is turned. A door
opens. Closes. A woman
waits at an upstairs window, watching a winter
sky which is opening its doors too. Snow
strikes the sill. Water hisses in a kettle.
Cats coil together on a rocking chair.

In the bedroom, a man arranges his shirts and ties.
A uniform. A coat. Razor and blades. His best
socks in neat fists. Through the open door
between them, a vanity

mirror catches a stalk of lamp-
light, doubles it, throws it back at her feet.
Between the mirror and the cast light, Sorrow sits.
Or Loss. Or Love. But far off. In a corner.
Attentive. Obedient. A good dog
waiting to be beckoned.

That At The Moment Of Departure
Each Gesture Fixes Itself

the sun-scrubbed walls of the bedroom

her straightening his collar and tie

him leaning, a last time, into the lavender scent of her hair

the baby fretting on her hip

the old hound baying at no one outside

him stepping onto the porch with his bags

all the geraniums nodding and waving

That There Are Moments Which, Utterly, Define You

This man who broke many years ago
    from a woman's body, still shawled
        in his scarlet caul of blood

and birth's debris, this man goes out
    from his wife and infant son
        to enter the camps of men.

His uniform terrifies her — pressed
    precisely, each creased seam straight
        as a razor, the epaulets and laurels

gleaming — even those gilt buttons are not
    innocent, are they? He cannot,
        attired thus, weep or show her his grief.

He waves and boards a train.
    Into the afternoon's gilt light, he travels:
        a man among other men.

He dozes. A whistle winds up and down
    in the stunned, descending dark.
        Cities, far off, gleam.

Overhead, a few sparse stars.
    All night, around him: other
        men whose names he does not know, strangers

clutching small valises or a woman's photograph,
    a locket or lock of hair.
        All night, like this, they ride together

rocked – side to side
    on the steel rails – deep
        in the bosom of Abraham.

That Even In Hell Our Shadows Would Be Eloquent

Three nights ago, the horned owl made
a watchtower of her loft.

Two mornings hence, his ironed shirt
slipped its hanger; the hallway mirror shivered.

Last night, in Baghdad, someone struck
a match — to light a lantern or a fuse?

And now the darkness that makes visible
the stars bares its claws at her.

She dreams tonight they find him, fallen
in a field, days-dead, a sparrow nested in his beard.

Yesterday's ghost still moves at will
through the ruined rooms of the house.

That Sometimes, In Order To See, You Must First *Not* See

Dilation. And a distortion so immense
    she must go, all morning, like the light-
blinded mole, the visible world gone
    ghastly-lit and blurry. To see
it requires dark lenses.
       When, in the wind, a black fan flutters
on the snowy stoop, she has to squint
    to make out bright threads
stitched along the riffling ribs:
    some new find the cat has
dropped, no doubt, at the door.
    She bends to lift it.
The eye says: *fan, embroidery.*
    The hand insists: *feathers, bones.*

What the tricked eye detects
    on the back of the severed
wing is light. And maybe that is
    what makes its way to her — whatever
light, true or false, is left to them now.
    He writes to her about those
who go into war like pennies into wells
    carrying on their backs the burden,
the unasked-for weight
    of someone else's dreams.

News of their dyings reaches her
    from a long way off and sometimes
she sees them moving from a valley of shadow
    to mountains brilliant with sun.
But the dead are always the dead, no matter
    how much light she throws over them.

Maybe death is, in the end, a mercy:
  like arriving at the shore of a strange sea,
a moored boat waiting and you stepping
  lightly into it, the white sails
unfurling, the setting-off, a faint sound
  like wind or warm surf breaking over the shimmering
hull and everything difficult, *everything*,
  behind you in the wake.

That Sometimes, And For No Good Reason, Someone You Love Is Spared

The last bullet in the last chamber
of the last pistol and the only survivor
walking down a hill towards home again
with what he held to and remembered:
the hem of his mother's blue dress,
the felled light in his father's eyes when she died,
the red tin lunchbox where, before they buried her,
the boy hid the nest and eggs he'd lifted from high in the sycamore,
the brown wren who hopped from limb to limb and watched him almost fall
as he climbed down again and, as he descended, the final cry of her in his ear.

That A Man, Returning, Will Not Be The Man Who Left

A world view: for months and months before he left
for war, he'd spoken of it as if to be without one
was to be godless. And then the planes. Four.

Forget a world view. What she wants
today is a table solid enough to set things on:
a lamp, a pitcher, a bowl of lemons.

She wants a dress the color of brandy.
She wants a black lace shawl.
A silk slip. A locket.

But Love, that tenderest tyrant of all,
fastens its necklace of flame
at her throat and she gives herself

over again to the lesser glory of who she is
with him: the glory of a bent spoke
and the rut it fell into.

She imagines him now
as he must have been then
in that other kingdom of men:

his doll-like face in its little uniform
of death; his shuttered eyes,
opening, closing;

and, underneath the ribs,
in place of an actual heart, the far-off
knocking of the guns that opened him.

That When You Say Now You See The Serpentness Of The World, Only The Grass Believes You

Her faith-fractured life; his hell-bent heart:
could anyone make a life out of this?

The ironwood rocker insists
on it and the man she almost loves tonight

sings to the teething boy on his lap.
Some nonsense about *hey-diddle-diddle.*

Something about a cat
and a fiddle. A dish. A spoon.

That More Separately Than You Enter It, You Exit The World

Then he died without a word to her.
    Monday noon he sopped the plate's rim
with a biscuit, finished off his jar

of buttermilk, pushed his chair from the table
    and walked, without a word, past her
through the screen door, out again into the far pasture.

For her, the day was boiling pots and mason jars, cross-
    hatches of light on scarred linoleum, fragments
of some old hymn she'd loved in her youth.

For him, the day was keeping again his own
    particular pact with long silence in far fields.
Occasionally, the belled sheep, bleating.

She saw him last from the kitchen
    window at twilight: his back against a fencepost,
hat resting on his lap, watching the westerly sun sink.

She said to herself, *Now, that's a man*
    with something on his mind.
She let him be.

Fireflies came out.
    Then the gibbous moon.
Then crickets lulled her to sleep.

By morning, he was so stiff
    the mortician had to set him upright
in the truck bed to get him to the morgue.

That Nothing Loves A Forest Like An Axe

Cover her mirrors, if you must;
    bring her a cake or casserole.

But do not offer her the thin tin
    cup of your pity.

Say you're sorry for her loss and she'll turn on you
    the stern granite of her face.

Was it she was happy those years with him?
    If so, why didn't she know it?

Maybe it's hard to know what you've built
    with a man until the roof's on fire.

Absurd, absurd, these things
    which will not stay in place.

Down the hall tonight, on what is barely
    a piano anymore, the boy plays

and, loudly, bellows, *You are*
    my sunshine, my only sunshine ...

a song he'd learned from her, so that something
    like praise rises in her finally for the errant

Craftsman who ordered the world
    and set its impermanence in her hands.

That Something Tries, In Pity Or Compassion, To Redeem You

After the funeral, the Amish chairmaker made the boy
    a rocking chair from scraps and painted it
blue: *a sorrow chair*, he'd called it.

Mornings now, the boy rocks wildly,
    mute and sober, in the yard. The postman
gives him a wide berth; farm boys gawk at him

from the gravel drive, then turn again
    to driving some mangy stray
down the road with stones and sticks.

When noon bells sound, he turns
    the chair around: his back to the street, his face
to the clapboard house, its neat rows

of yellow mums and the hay-stubbled fields beyond.
    And when the slow goat, Judas, nuzzles him,
the boy climbs on that bent back, blue

sorrow abandoned, and he rides,
    smiling and waving, through the afternoon,
silent as a Nazarene.

That You Arrive, Eventually, At The Insufficiency
Of *Just-Having Been*

The black-clad Amish walk, this August morning,
　　to the widow's farm for the belling of the new bull.

Their daughters sing, their dogs bark
　　sharply, their sons strike stones with long sticks.

They pass her solemn house, its drawn shutters, black
　　bunting bunched at the gatepost, the porch

rail, the door. A rogue almond tree burns
　　gold and bronze beside the barn; the killed hog

swings from a bough of oak. Stiff sheets
　　sail on the line. The cock, sour

in his spurs, crows at nothing
　　and rushes the dogs.

And in her garden going to ruin: the shameless
　　blue stars of the morning glory blaze.

That There Is No Accounting For
The Ways Of Love

Each stray that straggled home behind the man,
　　　each goat or mule or bull he'd bred, she'd had to
name, and had, as seriously as Adam had named
　　　beasts brought before him in that other almost-paradise.

And now she's got the whole of heaven
　　　and hell at her beck and call:
the old goat, Judas; the kittens, Faustus
　　　and Antichrist, who were

fathered by the stray gray Siamese
　　　Gideon whose mother, Magdalene, had been
her favored calico — a gentle lap-cat who,
　　　in the rage and fury of her heat,

had torn through three screen doors
　　　and climbed the chimney to slake
the wild thirst in her loins. And once, from the shelter,
　　　a pure-bred Labrador she'd named Pilate

whom she sometimes now sternly calls Pontius
　　　Pilate when she's cross with him
for driving off the mailman or chewing
　　　Faustus down again to a mewling maul of slobber.

So when the man had named their newborn
　　　boy himself, before she'd wakened from the after-
birthing stupor, she'd understood: wasn't that barnyard
　　　evidence of how the naming might have gone,

left to her? And now, the sober Amish neighbors
    returning to their own quiet farms,
she considers from a safe distance the final beast
    to be named — the newly-belled bull

calf — standing confused and cross in the noonday
    field of timothy and thistle, a hot sun
at his black back, flicking his tail
    at the blue-green halo of bottleflies.

She is wise enough today to see
    the rough beauty of the beast he is; also
foolish enough to love him more
    than all her much-loved other ones

for him having been the very one
    she had wrenched from his mother's
unyielding body into this world
    in the twilit hours of a vernal equinox.

Thus does she pronounce over him today his name:
    Lucifer. Lightbringer. 0h son of the dawn, 0h
bright and morning star for whom — even in the Gilead
    of a quiet pasture today — already the bright blade readies itself.

That Some Truths Can Only Be Known *Post Mortem*

Some twilights now she takes herself out to the fields.
She crosses over the fence and throws her arms

around the neck of the bull calf he was raising.
Through the rough fur and racket of his protest

she holds on fast and cries and loves at last
the rank animal smell of the beast:

that smell he'd carried home to her
each evening on his shirt, smell of animal

and alfalfa and sweat and him
that she'd laundered and laundered away.

That It Is Possible Some Things Might Live Beyond Their Moment In Time

As a parting gesture, she sets fire to the orchards.
She pulls down the stones of the garden wall
and unhinges the wooden door.

She leaves the house open to his enemies
who too will be disappointed
not to find him here.

In case something of him should return one day,
she sets out his favorite cup on the kitchen table.
Next to it: a singed bough

of applewood tied with a ribbon
from her hair: the last white
flag of her surrender.

HOUSE OF GATHERING

Psalm, From The Wayside

In parables, it is the place
the faithful are warned to stay away from: fallow
ground where sown seed won't take root among weeds and wild
thorns, ground where a righteous man might be so set upon
by thieves and thugs only a Samaritan could pull him
out of there again alive.

But Sunday morning, 5 a.m., the wayside, lit and close enough,
seems a likely stopping-place for someone who's been
driving, hard, away from failure, someone

with one more sweet dream curdling in the cup.
So I turn off, try not to think how familiar
it seems, like some scene from the late-night news:
the missing woman, traveling alone, was last seen here ....
The diner's almost-emptied now of everyone except two
yawning, grizzled truckers, the tattooed cook, and one

scrawny waitress singing along with a country song
on the radio: *... if I'm not over you
by the time I get to Georgia, I'll be Alabama-bound.*

A nice enough voice for a woman
who looks like hell has pitched its tent, a time or two,
in her face. She's what my people would call *fallen*, worldly,
a woman hard of countenance, the woman I've been
warned against, a cautionary tale: *There
but for the grace of God ....*

She brings me juice, refills
the truckers' mugs, asks if the road's been good
to them. She listens, nods and smiles.

I like her; I can't say why. Maybe
it's the way she carries the coffeepot, booth to booth,
as though she were bestowing blessings. Maybe it's that
she lists a little to the left — like I do —
when she's tired, and surely she is
tired. Maybe it's just that

she resembles a whore
who took me, and my four children, in
one night twenty years back when we had nowhere else to go.

It's warm in here, comfortable and strange
to sit, road-weary, raw, among the regulars who know
each others' names, and I am strangely comforted
for having arrived, a while,
among them. Everything
in order, wiped and gleaming: this

chipped formica table-top, white
paper napkins wrapped 'round the mismatched
silverware, two brown cups, upside-down, the handles

pointing east and west, the shakers
filled, the little boat of sugars, catsup and tabasco.
Okay, it isn't Paradise; but Lord, how can it be that
nothing in my life's prepared me
for how prepared I am for this?

Psalm, After The Fall From Remission

Remake me, Potter, or break me
into three final holy pieces: scatter me
knucklebone, eyelash, and tooth to the wind and rain.
Give what remains of me to the poor — called
last to every table save Death's.

For reasons worse than hunger, I'm driven
into bargaining again with You, the throttle thrown wide.

What a strange affliction being mortal is.
In one night, the camp of the body is made
or broken. I arm myself; I resist; I try
not to enter the one dark pass
where I will be taken.

Tonight my house is full with waking.
I, too, am full of a curtained hour I have not yet known.

When the sun rose today, this iron bed was bright with morning
and all the daily little blisses of ignorance. By the time the sun went down,
the world of the living was closed again to me, even the false light hope gives
off, and I lay feverish in cotton sheets so clean the rain was in them still.
Even the pillowslip was innocent of my undoing.

Conversation With My Body

I could leave you tonight,
    old bag of blood and trouble,
      old sack of pain.

I could get up and go out from you
    and travel ahead alone. I could
      go my own way and get there sooner.

Every bone of you would be left then
    to itself and its infidelities. Tonight
      I could leave you sitting here on the porch,

upright in the swing, and you
    would just go on hanging there, oblivious,
      a worn bell in the moonlit night.

The Long Way Back

for Sam

The road to hell is paved...and that's a road
down which I make my way to you again tonight, old
phantom of the doorstoop looped in darkness. Death's a song
I've lived in now so long it's become a wilderness, the way
home a footpath overgrown. Gone now

the old century, wild with its intentions,
into history books, yet that evening's a relic
still shattering under glass, the shards of it
lodged in me these thirty years. And that
thumbnail-sized crescent of cranium

which lodged itself under my collarbone
has been working its way heartward, year by year.
The surgeon says I'll have to have it
taken out lest it hit its mark.
I could tell him, if he'd listen, it has.

~

Nights now, as I'm nodding by a dying fire, the sharp
splinter of your undoing rises: a buried blade
deep as the green glade I used to wander
twilights, a dreamy girl in love
with solitude and trees; then voices, far-off;

and, beyond thinning pines and live oak, that
mossy clearing I stepped into as one boy took his
turn: he spun the silver cylinder and put the pistol
into his mouth. Nothing after that but three boys
running, bright terror, and the closing dark.

~

Your game. Your gun. Your brother.
Twice that year you hanged yourself.
Then it was razors and pills. And every time
doctors brought you the long way back
you cursed them, hard, for the resurrection.

I hear you have a little son now, a blue-eyed boy
you've named for him, and a daughter you named
after me: the awkward girl you'd mocked in school
who, splattered and stunned, held that shattered head together
while you stood by like a stone.

Sam, maybe we all have something to make up for,
some thing we just can't right, some penance
we'll never quite pay. I've meant, for years, to tell you: what I did
wasn't *courage*, like you thought. It was
just that I couldn't let go.

Psalm, After The Final Treatment

I shrug out of Death now easily as I do an overcoat
    and stand almost whole again this morning
        in a white shirt left to me by a man
            who died on my birthday, a cruelty
                I've not yet forgiven him for.

See, Lord, how I walk towards my life again
    as the ghost of *who-I-used-to-be* walks by me.
        The road stretches left, stretches right: no matter.
            Sooner or later the sky will blink
                and dim; the way will slip,

shadowed, lost again to me. So
    will I take it up once more, that
        which will be waiting for me
            there where I left it this morning
                on a hook by the door in or out.

Coming To This

What rotten luck. I have arrived
just as you are departing. Still,
if I may, I'd like a final word.

Listen; there is yet a little something
left to us: fields tilled and open to rain,
clouds dark with the coming

storm, a few fireflies at dusk.
Why not take what we love in our arms
tonight; why not dance 'til we drop,

together at last, into the maw of oblivion?
An old cradle sways in the dark.
You are in it, I see: father, mother, sisters, the lost

brother, that woman picking up
the dropped handkerchief of grief, the town
drunk, the drowned girl. And me. I am in it too.

So, whose hand has set us rocking?

After The Call About Your Heart

Fairbanks, Alaska, 1999

For once I do not think
of bears or the ill-tempered moose

who would willingly trample me
or the madman with his blood-

thirsty ax. Nor freezing to death. Nor the glittering
jaws of steel traps snapping. I'm reckless

in my terror tonight, shivering
high in the dark hills.

Below me, the city glows orangely in ice-
fog and light, like Saturn in its rings.

~

At the last lit window, my father's face
flutters a moment on the fickle wind of God's will.

Our God is a good God. He believes
this; I believe

in the dark wells of drowned cats, the sack-
cloth and ashes of love, rolled

gauze in the glovebox of my car, waiting,
like bridal beds, for the blood.

~

I imagine you there, Father, in Florida,
prepped, strapped to a gurney,

your chest and abdomen burnished with Betadine, a woman
like me wheeling you off to surgery, you half-gone already:

something run aground, something
dropped, like an awkward stone, into the well of oblivion.

You are done now with your prayers and God
is far beyond you; you are delivered

into the gloved hands and the chilly
antiseptic room, the monitor's

weep weep like an unstable bird
at the far edge of winter.

~

Tenderly someone lowers the light
to you; precisely, another brings the blade

to bear on the faulty heart; others
watch the oxygen, hang blood, keep you

in the merciful *nothingness* of sleep.
No one wants you now more than these.

Your angels, Father, are
with you.

~

Above me, the lights of heaven
flare: aurora borealis: solar storm: electromagnetic

winds blowing in from space. Across the valley,
at the Bed and Breakfast, tourists are coupling.

A strange fertility rite: to come to some desolate city
frozen at the top of the world, under storm-lights,

to conceive a child. Or maybe it's not
so strange. Maybe we're all conceived like this,

eye of the storm, center of God's wild plan, into a body
whose mysteries and failures we cannot comprehend.

Father, what's left to us now save this: to surrender
ourselves, to stand under heaven's storm,

swaying in its after-lights,
awe-struck and dumb?

Waiting For You, Father

1.

I have washed and pulled
a clean gown on, tied back
my mousy hair with a mist-blue ribbon.

The bells of St. Augustine's have rung
nine times and the boats have lowered their sails.

Twice now, I've said my prayers: once
because prayers please you and once as a poultice
over the old bruise in me called *God*.

Outside, the black night glitters.

2.

You must go now
the way all mortals go.
And so I spend your final hours

recalling the long, late evenings
of childhood, those twilights spent
searching star-stung skies as the whole

house seemed to lean, listening
with me, for some first sound
of your foot on the stair.

3.

I remember the slow drift of night,
fog off the river, the old dog
circling on the porch.

But why can I not recall now the ratchet and click
of the gate's hasp, that wide smile I knew
you would give me, that smile, each night,

I fell asleep waiting for?

Already I'm Almost There

When I left home at 18, the feral
cat that had followed me home one afternoon
left too. Each time I've visited since then,
my father insists that cat has come 'round again too.
I flinch each time he mentions him: that unnamed tom
my mother hated openly in the active, hostile way
I thought she hated me, too, in secret.
I'd learned, by then, to sit
through stony silences. To endure,
remembering Christ, his crown of thorns, his cross.

                                                  Not that
cat. He'd crawl inside the dryer — the one whose door fell open
like a broken jaw. He'd crouch inside that steel-blue barrel
and launch himself, full-claws, at her.
Or rather, at her stockings: expensive,
elastic, tight as a girdle so she might avoid,
in her later years, the shame
of varicose veins.

                         And then he'd dash — a streak of gunmetal
gray — out the open door, out again into the actual wilds of Florida.
For weeks sometimes, he'd be away.

                                   Those nights, drifting
towards sleep, instead of praying, I'd imagine him out there
among the crocodiles and copperheads, imagine him
picking his way through swamp mud, matted and reeking,
imagine him falling into the hands of boys who boasted of pranks
involving mailboxes and Roman candles,
matches and cats.

                         And I'd remember my mother
in her shredded hose, thin crimson slashes
on her shins and kneecaps where he'd made contact.
This, her eyes accused, *this is YOUR fault.*

And though the cat had
come after me on his own that afternoon, though I would
not — even in the wildest moment of my aching
loneliness then — have invited an animal, wild
or not, into that austere and godly household,
it had been me the cat had seen and followed
past the sewage treatment plant, through
Mrs. Barker's roses, down the gummy
asphalt of the street towards the manicured
lawn and whirling sprinklers of that house
on Janice Circle I used to call my home.
                              When every now
and then since his heart attack, my father phones and we are
suspended in that awkward silence after the first
hello, he'll say sometimes, "I miss that cat."
                              I understand:
this is close as he can get to *Come home; I need to see you*
because we are not a family who says such things. We're a family
who settles for *Pass the butter, please* and *Whose turn
to say the blessing?*
                              Last time I was home, I was 37,
all four children still in tow, my sons not yet
acne-pocked or interested in girls. I'm 49 now,
my father 70. And that would make the old tom
nearly 32. "Impossible;" I say,
"nine lives or not."
                              "Do all the math you want,"
my father says, "I trust my eyes. You come
home; he'll show."
                              Already I'm almost there,
under the hundred-year-old oaks, the falling

magnolia blossoms, around the corner, up the hill
to the top of Janice Circle and, in my shadow, two
tufted ears, two yellow eyes, one crooked
tail, four torn paws padding along behind,
heading home again: the ragged old
cat of my anger, brute beast
of my survival, the vicious
old cat of my love.

How It Goes

Each morning now, the Queen of the Damned goes off to work
at the local mortuary where she minds the phones
and, on slow afternoons, plays cards. It's a job
she likes. It pays the bills. Good
benefits. And because she doesn't have to go
below, she doesn't mind the great furnace there
and its irrefutable alchemy: *ashes*
to ashes, dust to dust. Her work
is accounts — receivable, payable — the lists
of names, the next of kin. It's not her
job to deal with the dead on the stainless
tables — the faces, unmade, remade — the bodies propped
properly into place again before the grief-stung families arrive.

∞

Upriver, the weary sockeye and king
have almost reached the spawning grounds,
returned — undone — to the waters of their making.

∞

Across town, a man
is dying. In a few days, or weeks,
he will have ceased to be. He will have left
behind, for good, the rented two-railed bed,
its bright blue bottom sheet, the catheter, diapers
and pills, the hinged tin of medicinal pot. Grown
children. A wife. All of us who've come. Who are
trying to hold him here one day more.
And all our reasons for doing so.

Because, In the End, We Are Given No Choice

Let the cup of the final hour
    Be delivered into his hands.

Let the phantom of regret
    Pay him a final visit.

Let the calendar's ritual of days
    Go forth now without him.

Let the last coins of the kingdom
    Cover his eyes.

Let any doubters left among us
    Touch the hem of his winding-sheet.

House Of Gathering

Time blows through and is done.
Those who have come to love him now have
come too late: see how the shadow moves
down at dusk to take the valley
in its arms. Hear the cry
of the corn, wheat whispering

It is time....

Listen, he says, *many
children are singing inside.*
He waves farewell; he enters
alone. The doors shut themselves
after him; the darkness pulls in close.
Only the lights in other houses burn.

Lessons From The Natural World

Look to the worm.
How well it is made. How
well its mouth accommodates the hook.
Thus hooked, how it complies, how it
takes on the crook and bend
of what runs through it in the end and goes on
writhing, a comely bait — little *come and get me,* little *here am I —*
how you too took on, hard, the shape of your dying.
And while you struggled, crooked, in your bed
Death ran you through from mouth to end
and snapped the thread that held you here.

You're gone. In your absence
how still the water's grown.

Departures: Last Flight From Fairbanks

Late and we were waiting – sixteen of us – with our coffee
and carry-ons, impatient for the call to board,
when a flight attendant appeared, apologizing.

I thought he said he hadn't felt right about sending *ice*
down the conveyor belt so he'd walked it
down himself. He placed, on the counter, a box:

insulated, sealed, orange-stickered, all four white sides
blackly lettered: *Human Eyes.* Around the box,
a hush gathered. Nothing else came near.

Whoever looked at it, looked quickly
away. When we boarded at last,
he carried the box

from the terminal, through the dim
tunnel, onto the bright plane. He held it
with both hands, in front of him, just inches

from his heart. He watched it in that way
a child watches what he is told to carry
carefully: no spilling; no dropping.

I would like to go out like that. I would
like to be borne one day from this
body, carried from the black

belly of the beast that mortality is,
into a last lifting-off. And, before that, I would
like to wait in some place where a hush gathers

around me one final time
while the world I have been part of
goes on as it always has: passing,

impatient, rushing to and fro, terminal
to terminal, in its long lit
corridors of sun and moon.

What I Am Waiting For

To linger longest, to be
still and quiet and good enough
until, one by one, the lights flicker
and go out, at last, in that house: doors
rusted and slipped from hinges, the porch
giving way to rain, old angers falling away to silence;

I'll approach it then, the rough-
hewn house of my childhood, emptied,
blind shutters banging in the wind;
I'll place my hand on the banister,
and climb the groaning stairs
to a room that was mine;

I'll lie down on the bed and watch
the stars come out again
through that crooked pane
where the safe world once glistened
and shone beyond me like the God I prayed to
who did not save me from anything;

Maybe then the knots in me
will come undone; maybe I will
be so whole for once I can sleep all night
though owls screech in the moony trees
and the weasels call out to each other
far off in the complicated dark.

Last Psalm

My Maker, my Creator, You
    will call me forth one day from this
bleak century. So say the prophets

    the doctors have become.

And when I come at last
    before You, You will see the glory
of this world, shardlike, in my eyes.

    And ever will I love

what I have loved in this life:
    the blossoming branch and the locust horde,
the beauty each is, and the terror.

NOTES

NOTES ON THE POEMS

"Judah's Lion"
1. Ezekiel's wheel, mentioned in the Old Testament (Ezekiel 1: 1 - 28), is the referent in an old spiritual which begins, *Ezekiel saw de wheel, way up in de middle ob de air.*
2. God's "eye roaming to and fro over the dark earth" is a reference to passages in scripture in which sinners are warned by the prophets that they will be called to accountability for their sins because God is a Being with His eyes turned, day and night, to both the good and the evil on earth.
3. "coming again and the unholy shall be judged and torn" is in reference to a passage from the Book of Revelations, which says the Messiah (the Lamb of God) will return at the end of days (as the Lion of Judah) to judge and punish the unholy ones.
4. "beautiful city of God" is from an old Baptist hymn, "Marching To Zion:"

"Beseeching The Lord Of Tooth And Claw"
"Destroying Angel" and "The Death Cup" are the colloquial names of wild mushrooms (*Amanita verna* and *Amanita virosa*) which are lethal to humans when ingested.

"The Body Of An Unidentified Woman Is Retrieved From The Jordan"
The Jordan River, here, is the river which runs through the Salt Lake Valley in Utah. In 2001, the riverbed was dry due to a five-year drought but, after a sudden rainstorm, it was swollen and ran in the treacherous undercurrents and eddies for which it has always been known. A woman was found, drowned in it. None of her personal belongings were recovered so she could not be identified. Neither did anyone come forward to claim her body. The coroner's autopsy notes suggested that the woman had recently given birth or was still nursing a child (evidence of lactation), was probably married (a gold band on her left hand), and that while the death looked like an accident (her left shoe was missing a heel), that suicide could not be ruled out because there was evidence of anti-depressants in her system. He suggested that she may have dressed hastily since she wore neither a slip nor undergarments under her dress. By the time I left Utah to return to Alaska, she had not been identified nor had her body been claimed.

"Gathering At The River"
"Joy cometh in the morning" is a quotation from Psalm 30:5. All other italicized lines are from an old Baptist hymn, "Shall We Gather At The River."

"Lucky"

In my childhood, it was widely rumored that, among the alligators of the Everglades, a fiercer reptile had been discovered: an African crocodile which had probably been illegally brought into the country and which had either escaped or had been released into the swamplands, a crocodile which swam among the Florida alligators and preyed on domesticated animals and lost children who wandered too close to the river banks.

"That This Is How It Begins"

Thou shalt not is a reference to the Ten Commandments; *if thine eye offend* is a reference to Christ's lesson to his disciples saying it was better to pluck out an eye if it causes one to sin than it would be to risk spending eternity in hellflames.

"That Every Love Song Becomes, In the End, a Lament"

0 Deus Otiosus is a Latin phrase which translates loosely into English as "O Do-Nothing God."

"That There Are Moments Which, Utterly, Define You"

"..rocked...deep in the bosom of Abraham" is a reference to an old spiritual, "Rock-A My Soul."

"Psalm, From The Wayside"

The poem makes reference to the parable of "The Good Samaritan" which is found in Luke 10: 30 - 37. In it, a man falls into the hands of thieves and robbers on a wayside road. When the wounded man's religious countrymen (Pharisees and Levites) pass him by and leave him for dead, a passing Samaritan shows compassion to the stranger.

"After The Call About Your Heart"

This poem mentions "a strange fertility rite." Each winter, Chinese couples come to the interior of Alaska during the darkest months (when the auroras are most visible and electrical activity in the heavens is strongest) in order to conceive a child under the storm-lights.

"How It Goes"

The Queen of the Damned, according to folk legend, is a living woman destined to always oversee the dyings of others though she herself is unable to die until her penance has been paid. (Legend never makes clear what her sin is.) In some civilizations, she is known as the *Shekinah*, a weeping, wandering woman who is said to embody the sorrow of God since He is incapable, in His holiness, of tears.

Toad Hall

Toad Hall is a not-for-profit writers' and artists' retreat in New Hampshire. Its purpose is to give creative people time, space, and freedom from day-to-day concerns. Attendees have come from all over the United States and from England and Scotland. Attendees have described their experience at Toad Hall as serious, joyous, productive, and often hilarious. Toad Hall Press is a logical addition to the enterprise. The press is dedicated to giving a forum to poets, artists, and writers. The press respects the sacred relationship between an artist/writer and the audience and aims to widen the opportunity for both to know each other.

The Toad Hall Press Editorial Board, Grace Cavalieri, Laura Orem, and Maria van Beuren, welcome submissions. Enquiries may be mailed to Toad Hall, 2330 Benton Road, North Haverhill, NH 03774, or e-mailed to mariac@indexing.com.

Toad Hall Press is indebted to J.H. Beall and Karren Alenier of **The Word Works** for their support and encouragement. Without them, the press might still be just a good idea.